Space
Guidebook

A ▬▬ easy to understand guide to energetic space cleansing.

Brynna Lyon

ISBN: 978-1-0899-5947-2

DEDICATION

This book is dedicated to all the teachers of my life and to all the people who have visited my home and healing space that have commented on how wonderful the energy is. You all inspired me to write this book!

TABLE OF CONTENTS

SPACE CLEARING GUIDEBOOK INTRO

This book is meant to be a fun and informative resource to help you utilize vibrational energy tools to mindfully create more peace and harmony in your life and space.

It is recommended to read through this guidebook before you attempt to clear your space, so that you are familiar with the tools and methods of use.

It should be noted that there is reference to tools that are used in exorcisms, however this guidebook does not specifically address clearing those energies.

There are many logical reasons or explanations in the physical world why things can feel off or why strange things can happen. Sometimes electric magnetic fields, hazardous and toxic materials, or a variety of other factors can create a definite disturbance within the energy of the space. However, there are forces and a whole unseen spiritual world around us that sometimes needs to be addressed.

If you are experiencing scary or odd occurrences; or are concerned about the possibility of ghosts, poltergeists, demons, or other low frequency energies, you need to consult a professional. It is a common myth that sage or other smudges will clear everything and that is not true! These types of circumstances and energies need to be handled carefully and are not something you should attempt to handle on your own. Clearing those types of energies requires a person with certain skill sets and spirituals gifts.

Shaman   **Psychopomp**   **Healer**   **Priest**

About Space Clearing

Space clearing is the unique process of clearing stagnant energies and re-setting the energy to a higher frequency. When our environment is at peace it promotes a space for us to also experience more peace. Space clearing de-stresses both the environment and the people living or working there. In this guide the words clearing, and cleansing will be interchangeable.

One of the major factors in our health and well-being that is often overlooked is the energy of the spaces we occupy. The land holds an energetic charge of everything that has ever taken place in it including traumatic events and the emotions from them along with any damage, vandalism or construction to the building or the land. These vibrations which energetically charge the molecules of the space get imprinted into the walls, furniture, landscape and everything in it and the space will continue to hold that frequency.

This energetic imprint results in the "feel" or vibe of the home or space and results in an unseen level of energetic debris, much like physical dust or cobwebs build-up. This causes the energy to be and feel stagnant, dull, heavy and many times extremely draining. Just like you would use the correct cleaning product to physically clean with, it is important to use the correct energetic cleansing products to produce the desired vibrational outcome.

The vibrational quality of a space has a direct influence on our energy field and what we are attracting into our life. We are consistently processing energetic information from our environment through our chakra system.

What are the Chakras?

Chakras are vortex-like subtle vital energy centers on the body which exist while the body is alive and disappear at death. Your Chakras work together as a system of reception, assimilation, and transmission of life energies in correspondence of the environment. The Chakras reflect and effect how we are processing energy on all levels physically, mentally, emotionally, and spiritually.

There are 7 major Chakras along the center line of the body and several more in other areas such as the hands and feet. Each Chakra corresponds to a major nerve plexus, gland system, color, body parts, various bodily process, and other major areas of our life. Each individual chakra focuses on a specific area such as survival, sex, power, love, communication, imagination, and spirituality. The chakras contain the programming and operating system of how we are handling these various aspects.

The function of the main Chakras is to properly integrate incoming energy and vitality from our environment within our energetic system to create changes within the physical body. It is ideal to have our energy freely flowing through our energetic pathways and free of blockages. The chakras allow us to energetically perceive each other and our environment by processing the surrounding energy through our system and by displaying how we are processing incoming energy through the transmission of our personal frequency. It is our personal frequency or our vibration that then attracts to us other similar type frequencies, thoughts, people, and circumstances that are in resonance with us or repels what is not in resonance.

TYPES OF CLEANSINGS

Clearing for Creation, Healing and Spiritual Intentions:

This is typically known as prayer or setting sacred space and is preformed using tools that reflect the intention of the prayer, healing, or creation. It is usually done in a specific area or room and can utilize a variety of tools.

Clearing Everyday Residue:

Our space, jewelry, furniture, crystals, clothes, etc. all collect energetic residue from the day's events, people, emotions, etc. Whenever we have a big emotional outburst such as fighting, crying, or yelling those vibrations create an energetic charge that lingers and gets imprinted into our items. Just like washing your hands it is important to cleanse your jewelry, crystals, and personal items often.

Physical Cleaning:

Physical matter and energy are both intertwined. Physically cleaning a space can do wonders to help shift energy. Physically cleaning should be done in combination with energetic cleansing.

Clear the clutter- You have an energetic connection to all your physical items. Anything that is just taking up space without bringing you joy is just weighing you down. It makes the energy very heavy and stagnant. It also keeps you an emotional and mental prisoner to your past. Your ability to be productive and think clearly is also influenced by the state of the environment you live or work in. An environment that is full of clutter and highly disorganized creates scattered and chaotic energy. It is overwhelming to your energy system and is not helpful for being able to focus or think clearly.

We are meant to live in the present moment. Some of our possessions are not even a true reflection of who we are anymore in this present moment. We can honor our past and especially our past loved ones but that does not require us to be attached to physical items that do not bring us joy or serve a purpose. Items that belonged to our loved ones who are deceased, are not our loved ones. They are items associated with them and their memory. Sometimes keeping too many of those items can keep us trapped in grief and guilt, instead of allowing us to fully release and truly connect with the present moment and our hearts. Our hearts are where the love & memories of our lost loved ones truly remain, not the item. We must create space for healing and for new and better to come in.

Do you want to manifest something new in your life? For example, a new lover? Ask yourself, "Does the energy of my space reflect that I have room for that in my life?" If your bedroom is jam packed full, unorganized, and clothes are everywhere… you don't have room! However, you can shift that energy by cleaning up and organizing. Make space in the closet and on a nightstand for another person. This is closer in vibrational alignment with your desires and it shifts the energy towards more thoughtfulness and care towards yourself and what you already have. You get more of wherever you put your focus and intention towards.

It is vital to do the physical clearing and cleaning work if you want to truly clear out stagnant energy and get things moving. If the physical clearing and cleansing is not done, then the environment will return to and stay at the same frequency regardless of any energetic cleansing that is done.

On a positive note, once a space is cleared of clutter, arranged, and decorated in a way that is ideal for great energy flow, it is easy to maintain the good vibe. We all deserve to live a home we love being in and that feels amazing to us.

It is highly recommended to use natural cleaning products. There are several non-toxic and natural products that are better for both your health and the environment. Many cleaning products can easily be made using inexpensive items you can easily find in the grocery store such as white vinegar and baking soda. Essential oils are also an increasingly popular resource for natural cleaning. Tea tree oil, lemon and numerous other essential oil blends not only do a fantastic job with cleaning but also can help repel rodents and insects along with managing mold and mildew.

Complete Clearing:

This type of clearing does not need to be done all the time because it completely clears the space of both positive and negative energy and leaves it a neutral space. It is typically done to an entire home, building or office.

This type of clearing should be done:
* When you sell or move to a new home or business location
* Experience odd occurrences or traumatic events
* After any remodeling, construction, demolition, or property damage to home or land.
* When starting a new project or after a major life change such as a divorce, change in career, or the death of a loved one to clear the way for a solid foundation & positive new beginning.

Clearing Your Energy Field:

Your energy field or aura is consistently exposed to all types of energy and will absorb some of that energy. If not cleansed or dispelled, it can build up and can start to manifest as negative thoughts, sickness, or the attraction of unpleasant people or circumstances. Your aura contains many different parts such as your chakras, energetic cords, layers of the aura, meridian system, and much more. Clearing and healing all those things take time as they are always changing as you develop and live your life. We are always on our healing journey. When we say aura cleanse, what we mean is, a way to help rid you of as much debris as possible before it manifests.

TOOLS USED IN SPACE CLEANSINGS

Bells, Gongs, Rattles, Tuning Forks:

Due to their powerful vibration's bells, gongs and rattles have an amazing ability to break up stagnant and resistant energy and get energy flowing again. Tuning forks are specially tuned to certain notes which have the capability to manipulate and entrain energy to the same vibration to achieve a desired result such as being grounded, feeling relaxed, feeling stimulated, etc.

Voice, Stomping and Clapping:

Your voice is a powerful tool. It can be used in several different ways. First is in setting intentions and filling a space with the vibration of a word or an intention. Second, you can use your voice to break up stagnant or resistance energy simply by making sounds that break things apart. These can be sounds like a bomb makes, firecrackers, growling, splattering, clicking tongue, and much more. Another great way to bust up energy is by stomping or clapping.

Energetic Cleansing Spray:

This spray is easy to make and does a remarkable job of quickly cleansing everyday objects such jewelry, crystals, and personal items. It is a master cleanser of emotional outbursts and disturbances. It can be sprayed in the air or on objects such as beds and furniture. You can even spray yourself!

How to Make an Energetic Cleansing Spray:
Use a brown or colored glass spray top bottle filled with distilled or filtered water and add 1 drop Bach Flower Rescue Remedy and 4 drops Crab Apple Bach Flower Remedy. Shake well before use. Not for internal use.

Tea:

One old time favorite Aura Cleanse method is a tea bath. Tea has a multitude of health benefits along with its purifying and detoxifying properties. Use 4-5 tea bags of black tea and put them into the bathwater as the tub is filling. Using tea bags is an easy way to fetch them out of the water for easy clean-up. The bath water's color does not need to be super dark to be effective. Rinse your body off before you leave the bath, so that you do not stain your towels. Remove the tea bags and rinse your bathtub afterwards.

Salt:

Salt has long been used as a purifying and preservative agent. Some people like to boil or soak their crystals and jewelry in saltwater to cleanse them. This is an effective method. However, a word of caution that you can damage some crystals/gemstones and jewelry depending upon the properties of the gemstone as some do not react well to saltwater or water and can be damaged. Please inform yourself before using this method.

Taking a sea salt bath is great for removing lingering energy within your energy field. Epsom salt is another great choice as it helps with a multitude of ailments, is detoxifying, and supplies us with magnesium. Mixing essential oils with salt and then adding it to the bathwater is a wonderful treat. Be sure you are aware of how to safely use essential oils and which oils are safe for topical use. If you have any medical conditions, please make sure it is safe for you to take a salt bath.

Water:

One quick and easy way to neutralize energy is rinsing with water. It is vital for anyone doing massage, body work, healing, caregiving, or constantly touching people to always wash their hand before and after working with clients to discharge any energetic residue. Taking a shower can help neutralize the energetic residue of the day also. If you are easily over-stimulated, deal with anxiety, or feel emotionally charged (such as getting agitated) then a shower can be a good resource. You can also rinse some stones and jewelry with water as a quick way to clear residue. Be sure you are aware of which stones will not be damaged by water. If you do massage or bodywork it is important to spray and wipe your table down after each person for physical sanitation reasons and to dispel energetic charges from the healing and emotional release work.

Feathers:

Feathers are a sacred tool in many tribal and indigenous communities. They are used during cleansings, blessings, healings, and ceremonies. Feathers are often ceremonially cleansed and single feathers are usually wrapped at the end and can also be made into a feather fan. If you have been given a feather or find one outside, please treat it with respect and do not place your feathers on the ground. Any feather or fan that comes from a finding a dead bird should absolutely be cleansed and blessed to honor the bird's spirits and to rid any traumatic energy lingering from its death.

Every type of bird carries a unique "medicine", messages, lessons, and symbolism. It is a high honor to be given or receive a feather in many beliefs and cultures. Feathers used to smudge should be of a good size and will belong to larger size birds. Turkey feathers are good to use for smudging.

In the United states it is illegal to own certain types of bird feathers, regardless of how they are acquired, unless you are of a native ethnicity and have obtained prior permission for religious purposes. Please be mindful and inform yourself of the laws regarding which feathers are illegal.

Smudge:

There are several types of herbs that when burnt have cleansing and purifying effects on the environment. Smudges are also used in prayer, manifestation, healing, meditation, spiritual practices, and numerous rituals due to their profound ability to produce beneficial effects on the mind, body, and spirit. Each type of smudge carries a unique vibrational property that can drastically shift energy and create new experiences and opportunities.

Always use a Smudge Bowl or Abalone Shell!

How to Use Smudge:

To burn smudge, hold the smudge stick or wood in your hand at a 45-degree angle and light the end so that there is a flame or smoke. Gently shake or blow on the smudge until it is only smoking. You can hold the smudge in your hand or use a smudge bowl. Be sure you have the bowl with you because as it burns, you will have ash droppings. Be mindful of smoke detectors. You do not need to use a ton of smoke. Gently allow the smoke to cover your items or space. When you are done, press the smudge into the smudge bowl until you are sure it is no longer smoking.

Types of Smudges

White Sage:

White Sage is used for cleansing and purification. It clears both negative and positive energy leaving it a neural space. It neutralizes the build-up of harmful ions and is a powerful antiseptic that can purify the air of 94% of harmful bacteria for up to 24 hours. Diffusing an essential oil afterwards, is helpful with the intense smell. You should smudge any used furniture or jewelry entering your space with white sage.

Blue Sage:

Blue Sage is also used for cleansing and purification although it is not as strong smelling as white sage. Blue Sage is used for spiritual strength and is good for helping to clear areas of hateful emotions. It can be helpful in healing rituals and great to prepare a sacred space to use for things such as meditation.

Palo Santo Wood:

This wonderful smelling wood has been used for centuries by shamans and healers in prayer and healing ceremonies. It is known as "holy wood". Palo santo has a grounding and focusing effect and can help increase creativity, productivity, and bring abundance. Palo Santo is rich in brain-

oxygenating terpenes such as limonene and a-terpineol. Palo Santo transmutes negativity into love and light. Use Palo Santo for meditation to deflect and repel negative energies and create a high vibration. If you have special prayer requests, healing needs, or need a special blessing then burn Palo Santo and clearly state your intentions and prayers.

Sweet Grass Braid:

Sweet grass smudge is prepared as beautiful braid and smells quite lovely and uplifting. Sweet grass is burned primarily to usher in positive energy and as a protection shield of angels and our ancestors. When starting a new venture burn sweet grass to help let go of what is no longer serving you and bring in new and fresh energy.

Cedar:

Cedar is used for creating sacred space, healing and for protection. It is commonly used in sweat lodge ceremonies for purification and attraction of good spirits. Also used in exorcisms, clearings of negative entities and for purposes of banishing and spell breaking.

Juniper:

Use Juniper to usher in new love, healing sexual issues, fertility, increase libido and romance. It protects against harmful and negative thoughts and energies while promoting overall good health. Juniper is burned in healing rituals for diseases from spiritual attachments or entities.

Pine:

Pine is used for increasing prosperity and abundance, ushering in joy, purification, healing, protection against illness, and is used in exorcisms. This powerful emotional healer gives a great boost of energy to move through difficult situations while expelling negative energy and restoring self-confidence and self-respect. Pine will help to quickly get things moving and unblocked.

Yerba Santa:

Yerba Santa, also known as the holy herb, has a pleasant and uplifting scent. It is a wonderful to use for love and beauty. Yerba Santa is great for purification and helps with respiratory issues as well as releasing emotional pain and grief stored in the heart chakra. Use Yerba Santa for protection and to promote personal empowerment and well as setting boundaries.

Mugwort (Black Sage):

Mugwort is known as the "dream weaver" for its ability to stimulate vivid and prophetic dreams. It is a mild psychoactive herb and is used to assist in opening the 3rd eye chakra (chakra 6) to enhance psychic awareness and contact with the spirit world. It can aid in dream work, meditation, astral travel, spiritual protection and growth, and intuitive development. Smudge your car for safe travel. Use for very dark energies and protection. Also used in exorcisms, clearings of negative entities and for purposes of banishing and spell breaking.

Eucalyptus:

Eucalyptus brings a clean, purifying, refreshing vibe. It is great for those suffering from colds, respiratory, and sinus issues. It fosters clarity and positive moods and mindsets. Wonderful in ushering in fresh energy. It is great for setting personal sacred space in an area where you may need some solitude.

www.HealingwithB.com

Tools to Shift and Recharge Energy

After a complete clearing you will want to recharge your space. These tools can also be used to shift energy throughout the day.

Candles:
Candles are an extremely easy way to uplift an environment and recharge space. Using soy or beeswax candles is a good option for people with allergies or respiratory issues and those who want to avoid toxins. Candles can be used to also create a very inviting and cozy environment as well as setting the mood for romance or passion.

Fresh Air & Sunlight:
Fresh air and sunlight are both important in recharging and shifting energy. Sunlight has an extremely beneficial effect overall. Let the sun in!

Himalayan Salt Lamps:

Himalayan salt lamps help purify the air, elevates mood, reduces anxiety, reduces electromagnetic radiation, eases allergies and asthma, reduces airborne infections, and has a positive effect on the respiratory system.

Incense:

Incense comes in the form of a gum, resin, cone, or stick that is an aromatic material and releases fragrant smoke when burned. Use with caution if you have respiratory issues. Incense has long been used in meditation, worship ceremonies, used to honor ancestors or work with ancestor energy.

* **Sandalwood:** is a common incense used in meditation as it promotes mental clarity and is calming and relaxing. It also provides several health benefits and is a natural aphrodisiac.

* **Frankincense Resin:** Highly spiritual in nature, frankincense is known for its ability to heighten communication with the creator/spirit, reduce stress and anxiety, Uplifts the spirit, helps with depression, and is a master healer. Use during meditation and healing ceremonies.

* **Myrrh Resin:** Burned as incense for purification, exorcism, protection and healing. Commonly used in funerary rituals and as anointing oil in many religions. Myrrh helps cope with loss and helps heal the body, mind, and spirit after devastation.

Essential Oils:
Diffusing essential oils are an easy and effective way to quickly shift the vibe of the environment along with having a profound effect on our moods and emotions. Before using essential oils please inform yourself about essential oil safe usage. Use a therapeutic grade oil for best results.

Spiritual/Meditation: Frankincense, Palo Santo, Patchouli, Sandalwood, Lavender, Myrrh, Hyssop, Rose

Uplifting: Lemon, Orange, Lemon Grass, Palo Santo, Frankincense, Jasmine, Ylang Ylang, Wintergreen, Juniper, Lime, Neroli, Rose

Grounding: Valerian, Cedar Wood, Pine, Rosemary, Cypress, Balsam Fir, Fennel

Relaxing: Lavender, Valerian, Clary Sage, Chamomile, Juniper, Mastrante, Hinoki

Stimulating: Peppermint, Clove, Cinnamon, Rosemary, Orange, Black Pepper, Wintergreen, Lime, Neroli, Palma Rosa

Protection: Angelica, White Angelica, Lavender, Sage, Cedar

Plants: A nice healthy plant or fresh cut flowers can bring in refreshing and balancing energy to most every space. It is important to research the type of indoor plant that will thrive in that individual space according to the amount of light needed. Be sure to get rid of dead flowers and keep your plants healthy.

HOW TO DO A COMPLETE SPACE CLEARING

You may not need to do every step in this process depending on your intention and circumstances at that time.

1) Evaluate the space.

a) What is the over-all vibe of the space? How is the energy flowing and where are there energetic issues or places where the energy is not flowing properly? Is any non-optimal energetic flow caused by architectural layouts, geometrical stress, structural damage, electric-magnetic radiation, or bad Feng Shui? Come up with a plan to address these things.

b) What is the history of the space? What events have taken place in the past? What have the past occupants been like? What is the surrounding environment and occupants? Has there been destruction, vandalism, or demolition to the surrounding property especially trees and wildlife? Some of these may require healing of the land which is different than space clearing and you should consider a professional. You will also want to use this information to determine what type of tools to use.

c) Am I able to handle any difficult energies that may be present in this space? Possible situations that could result in difficult or low frequency energies are frequent drug/alcohol/tobacco/pot use, sexual activity involving several different partners, abuse/trauma, death, depression or frequent emotional disharmony, frequent fighting, or yelling.

2) Physically clean and organize.

If you are doing a clearing after a major life change such as a death or are moving, go ahead and clear the space just as it is. Sometimes the physical cleaning and organizing will be a process.

3) Prepare your tools. You will need:

a) Something to breakup any resistant or stagnant energy such as a bell, rattle, or your voice.
b) White sage and other smudges you want to use, lighter, smudge bowl and feather if wanted.
c) Things you are going to use to recharge the energy.

4) Open the windows and doors! Open closets, drawers, and jewelry holders.

Pull out your crystals and jewelry if possible.

5) Center and ground yourself. Ask your spiritual connection to be present. Connect with the space and pay attention to any intuitive messages you receive.

6) Smudge

In each room announce your intention and break up any resistant or stagnant energy. Generally, you will use white sage in a complete clearing and/or any other smudges that are appropriate. Be sure to remain centered and grounded during this process. Start on the outside border of the room and work your way in. Move the smudge or smudge bowl up and down and gently use the feather to fan the smoke (if your using a feather) so that the smoke covers all the areas and items. Do your best in places such as closets and under beds. Pay special attention to trace the frame of mirrors, windows, and doors. If possible, smudge your jewelry and crystals. If the smudge is no longer smoking just light it again and continue. It is especially helpful to also smudge the perimeter of your property. You should also smudge yourself at the end by waving the smudge around yourself, your head, body, and under your feet.

Push the smudge against the smudge bowl to put out!!

7) Recharge the space

Allow a little time for the air to come in. Go to each room and recharge the energy by lighting candles, use incense, diffuse essential oils or any other things you choose. Allow as much sunlight into each room as possible. When you are ready you can close all the windows, doors, drawers, etc.

8) Consciously create your space

Every individual room or space has its own unique function and feel. Decorate and beautify each space to reflect the type of activities and energy you wish it to be. It is important to decorate personal spaces with items that reflect who you are in the current moment and that feel good to you. It is highly recommended to work with a Feng Shui consultant to assure good energy flow in your home or business. You can also utilize Feng Shui books to help you find creative ideas and effective solutions for tricky areas.

For each room it is important to determine what the purpose of the space is. Most likely your space is going to be a defined room like a bedroom, bathroom, kitchen, and office. So, you will have an idea who resides or spends time in the space and what activities take place there. You will want to choose colors and items that are appropriate for the space.

For instance, if you are working on your bedroom then the purpose of a bedroom is for sleep, relaxation, and love making. Putting a piece of exercise equipment or a work desk in the bedroom is not in alignment with the purpose of that space and is inviting active energy and your work into your bedroom. How is that energy going to affect your sleep quality, your love life or even the connection with your partner? It is important to consider these things when creating your space.

ABOUT THE AUTHOR

Brynna Lyon
Certified Energy Therapist & Vibrational Medicine Teacher
www.HealingwithB.com

Brynna Lyon is the owner of Spiritual Journey Energy Healing Training located in Sumner, Washington. She is a Certified Energy Therapist & Vibrational Medicine Teacher with a 560-hour Diploma in the art and science of energy healing and vibrational medicine from the Earthwalk Institute of Healing Arts. With over 15 years of experience, she offers a variety of training programs and services for both personal healing and professional practitioners. Brynna has integrated all her life experiences into her work including an extensive background as a certified nursing assistant, personal assistant, household manager, small business coach, hospice care, and an executive director of a home healthcare agency.

Brynna has a great love for humanity and is passionate about helping people to get "unstuck" and into alignment with their true path. She loves educating people about energy healing and empowering them with tools they can use for their own wellness. "This is my passion, soul's purpose and life's mission."

Music, dancing, and singing has always been among Brynna's favorite activities. She feels both dancing and singing is an expression of her soul and a way for her to connect to the divine. Brynna also enjoys being out in nature and is a great supporter of taking care of and protecting our planet, environment, and wildlife. Spending time with friends and family, good food, sunshine, laughter, live music, and street fairs and festivals makes her heart happy.

Much Love,
Brynna Lyon

Made in the USA
Columbia, SC
20 March 2024

33378377R00018